CUMBRIA LIBRARIES
3 8003 04828 9011
KT-547-661

SILLY VERSE FOR KIDS

…KE MILLIGAN was born at Ahmednagar in India …1918. He received his early education in a tent …he Hyberabad Sindh desert and graduated from …here, through a series of Roman Catholic Schools in India and England, to the Lewisham Polytechnic. H… served for five years in the Royal Artillery, t…ing part at the landings in Algiers (during his …vice in Africa he was mentioned in Dispatches) …d in the invasion of Sicily at Salerno, before …eing wounded at Monte Cassino. Once out of the …vices, Spike Milligan plunged into the world of …w business, having been drawn to it by his first …ge appearance, at the age of eight, in the nativity … of his Poona convent school. He began his …s a band musician before becoming famous …, a poet, a humorous script writer and …s the originator and writer of the …w.

…ied in February 2002 at the age

SILLY VERSE FOR KIDS

SPIKE MILLIGAN

PUFFIN POETRY

PUFFIN BOOKS

UK | USA | Canada | Ireland | Australia
India | New Zealand | South Africa

Puffin Books is part of the Penguin Random House group of companies
whose addresses can be found at global.penguinrandomhouse.com.

puffinbooks.com

First published by Dennis Dobson in *Silly Verse for Kids*,
A Dustbin of Milligan and *The Pot Boiler*
1959, 1961, 1963

Published in Puffin Books 1968
Reissued in this edition 2015
003

Copyright © Spike Milligan, 1959, 1961, 1963
All rights reserved

The moral right of the author/illustrator has been asserted

The poems on pp. 61–69 are printed by permission of Tandem Books

Set in Baskerville MT
Printed in Great Britain by Clays Ltd, St Ives plc

A CIP catalogue record for this book is available from the British Library

ISBN: 978-0-141-36298-4

www.greenpenguin.co.uk

MIX
Paper from
responsible sources
FSC
www.fsc.org   FSC® C018179

Penguin Random House is committed to a
sustainable future for our business, our readers
and our planet. This book is made from Forest
Stewardship Council® certified paper.

This book
is dedicated to
my bank balance

Contents

Foreword

Most of these poems were written to amuse my children; some were written as a result of things they said in the home. No matter what you say, my kids think I'm brilliant!

S. M.

String

String
Is a very important thing.
Rope is thicker,
But string,
Is quicker.

P.S. The meaning of this is obscure
That's why, the higher the fewer.

Mary Pugh

Mary Pugh
Was nearly two
When she went out of doors.
She went standing up she did
But came back on all fours.
The moral of the story
Please meditate and pause:
Never send a baby out
With loosely waisted draws.

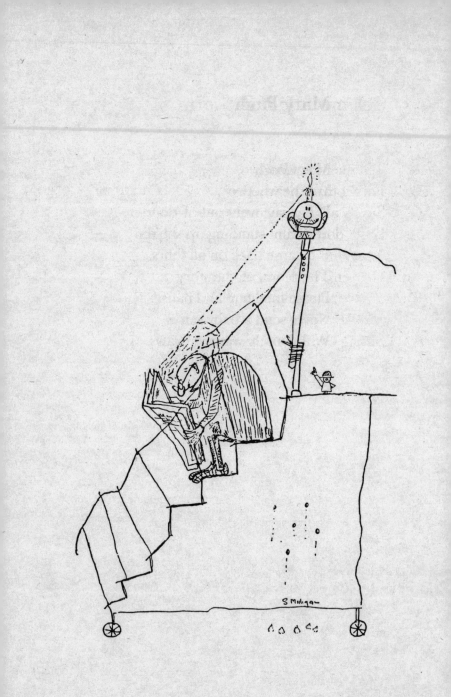

Tell me little woodworm

Tell me little woodworm
Eating thru the wood.
Surely all that sawdust
Can't do you any good.

Heavens! Little woodworm
You've eaten all the chairs
So *that's* why poor old Grandad's
Sitting outside on the stairs.

Hipporhinostricow

Such a beast is the Hipporhinostricow
How it got so mixed up we'll never know how;
It sleeps all day, and whistles all night,
And it wears yellow socks which are far too tight.

If you laugh at the Hipporhinostricow,
You're bound to get into an awful row;
The creature is protected you see
From silly people like you and me.

I've never felt finer

'I've never felt finer!'
Said the King of China,
Sitting down to dine –
Then fell down dead – he died he did!
It was only half past nine.

Said the General

Said the General of the Army,
'I think that war is barmy'
So he threw away his gun:
Now he's having much more fun.

Two children (small)

Two children (small), one Four, one Five,
Once saw a bee go in a hive.
They'd never seen a bee before!
So they waited there to see some more.
And sure enough along there came
A dozen bees (and all the same!)
Within the hive they buzzed about;
Then, one by one, they all flew *out*.
Said Four: 'Those bees *are* silly things,
But *how* I *wish* I *had* their *wings*!'

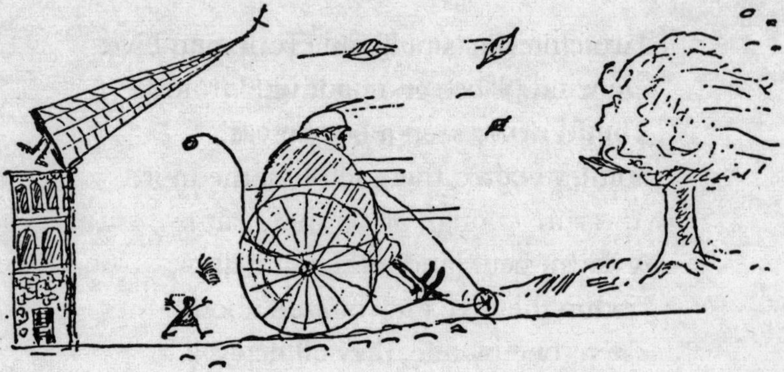

Granny

Through every nook and every cranny
The wind blew in on poor old Granny;
Around her knees, into each ear
(And up her nose as well, I fear).

All through the night the wind grew worse,
It nearly made the vicar curse.
The top had fallen off the steeple
Just missing him (and other people).

It blew on man; it blew on beast.
It blew on nun; it blew on priest.
It blew the wig off Auntie Fanny –
But most of all, it blew on Granny!!

Hello Jolly Guardsman

'Hello Jolly Guardsman
In your scarlet coat:
It reaches from below your tum
To half way up your throat.

'Tell me jolly Guardsman
When you're off parade
What kind of clothes do you put on?'
'Civvies I'm afraid.'

Today I saw a little worm

Today I saw a little worm
Wriggling on his belly.
Perhaps he'd like to come inside
And see what's on the Telly.

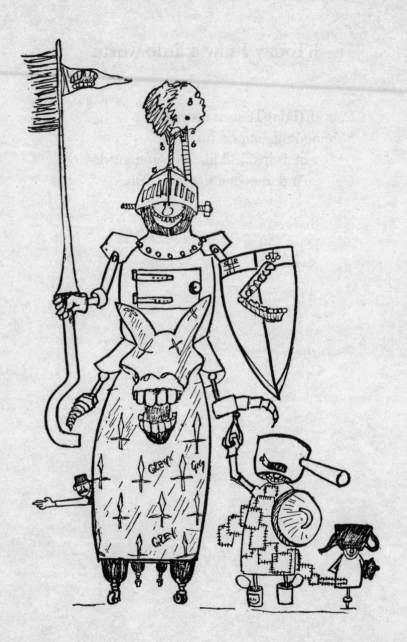

Teeth

English Teeth, English Teeth!
Shining in the sun
A part of British heritage
Aye, each and every one.

English Teeth, Happy Teeth!
Always having fun
Clamping down on bits of fish
And sausages half done.

English Teeth! HEROES' Teeth!
Hear them click! and clack!
Let's sing a song of praise to them –
Three Cheers for the Brown Grey and Black.

Look at all those monkeys

Look at all those monkeys
Jumping in their cage.
Why don't they all go out to work
And earn a decent wage?

How can you say such silly things,
And you a son of mine?
Imagine monkeys travelling on
The Morden-Edgware line!

But what about the Pekinese!
They have an allocation.
'Don't travel during Peke hour',
It says on every station.

My Gosh, you're right, my clever boy,
I never thought of that!
And so they left the monkey house,
While an elephant raised his hat.

Can a parrot

Can a parrot
Eat a carrot
Standing on his head?
If I did that my mum would send me
Straight upstairs to bed.

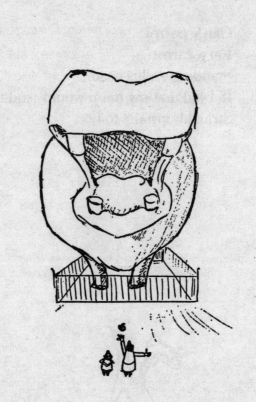

I'm not frightened of Pussy Cats

I'm not frightened of Pussy Cats,
They only eat up mice and rats,
But a Hippopotamus
Could eat the Lotofus!

Down the stream the swans all glide

Down the stream the swans all glide;
It's quite the cheapest way to ride.
Their legs get wet,
Their tummies wetter:
I think after all
The bus is better.

On the Ning Nang Nong

On the Ning Nang Nong
Where the Cows go Bong!
And the Monkeys all say Boo!
There's a Nong Nang Ning
Where the trees go Ping!
And the tea pots Jibber Jabber Joo.
On the Nong Ning Nang
All the mice go Clang!
And you just can't catch 'em when they do!
So it's Ning Nang Nong!
Cows go Bong!
Nong Nang Ning!
Trees go Ping!
Nong Ning Nang!
The mice go Clang!
What a noisy place to belong,
Is the Ning Nang Ning Nang Nong!!

The Land of the Bumbley Boo

In the Land of the Bumbley Boo
The people are red white and blue,
They never blow noses,
Or ever wear closes,
What a sensible thing to do!

In the Land of the Bumbley Boo
You can buy Lemon pie at the Zoo;
They give away Foxes
In little Pink Boxes
And Bottles of Dandylion Stew.

In the Land of the Bumbley Boo
You never see a Gnu,
But thousands of cats
Wearing trousers and hats
Made of Pumpkins and Pelican Glue!

Chorus

Oh, the Bumbley Boo! the Bumbley boo!
That's the place for me and you!
So hurry! Let's run!
The train leaves at one!
For the Land of the Bumbley Boo!
The wonderful Bumbley Boo-Boo-Boo!
The Wonderful Bumbley BOO!!!

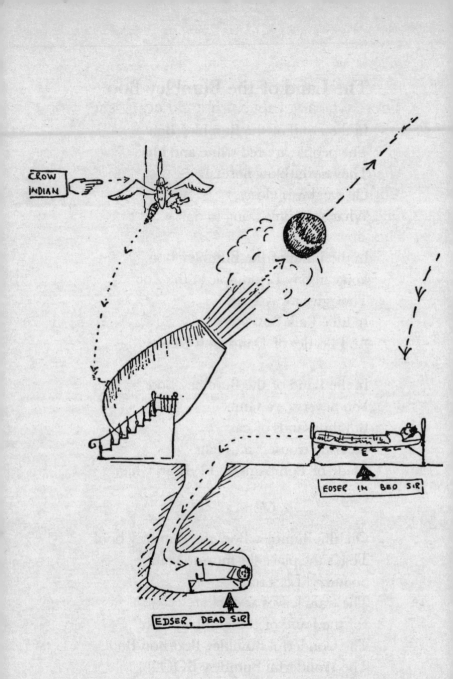

CROW INDIAN

EDSER IN BED SIR

EDSER, DEAD SIR

There was a young soldier called Edser

There was a young soldier called Edser
When wanted was always in bed sir:
One morning at one
They fired the gun
And Edser, in bed sir, was dead sir.

You must never bath in an Irish Stew

You must never bath in an Irish Stew
It's a most illogical thing to do
    But should you persist against my reasoning
    Don't fail to add the appropriate seasoning.

Hello Mr Python

Hello Mr Python
Curling round a tree,
Bet you'd like to make yourself
A dinner out of me.

Can't you change your habits
Crushing people's bones?
I wouldn't like a dinner
That emitted fearful groans.

The Bongaloo

'What is a Bongaloo, Daddy?'
'A Bongaloo, Son,' said I,
'Is a tall bag of cheese
Plus a Chinaman's knees
And the leg of a nanny goat's eye.'

'How strange is a Bongaloo, Daddy?'
'As strange as strange,' I replied.
'When the sun's in the West
It appears in a vest
Sailing out with the noonday tide.'

'What shape is a Bongaloo, Daddy?'
'The shape, my Son, I'll explain:
It's tall round the nose
Which continually grows
In the general direction of Spain.'

'Are you *sure* there's a Bongaloo, Daddy?'
'Am I sure, my Son?' said I.
'Why, I've seen it, not quite
On a dark sunny night
Do you think that I'd tell you a lie?'

My sister Laura

My sister Laura's bigger than me
And lifts me up quite easily.
I can't lift her, I've tried and tried;
She must have something heavy inside.

Failure

I'm trying to write the longest first line that poetry has ever had,
For a start that wasn't bad,
Now here comes a longer oneeeeeeeeeeeeeeeeeeeeeeeeeeeeeeeeeeeeeeeee
I know I cheated:
It was the only way I could avoided being defeated.

I once knew a Burmese horse

I once knew a Burmese horse:
Of course
He didn't know he was a horse;
But I knew Jim
So I told him –
Now he knows
And so, I close.

My daddy wears a big black hat

My daddy wears a big black hat;
He wears it in the street
And raises it to lady folk
That he perchance should meet.
He wears it on a Sunday
And on a Monday too.
He never wears it in the house,
But only out of doors.

Maveric

Maveric Prowles
Had Rumbling Bowles
That thundered in the night.
It shook the bedrooms all around
And gave the folks a fright.

    The doctor called;
    He was appalled
    When through his stethoscope
    He heard the sound of a baying hound,
    And the acrid smell of smoke.

Was there a cure?
'The higher the fewer,'
The learned doctor said,
Then turned poor Maveric inside out
And stood him on his head.

    'Just as I thought
    You've been and caught
    An Asiatic flu –
    You musn't go near dogs I fear
    Unless they come near you.'

Poor Maveric cried.
He went cross-eyed,
His legs went green and blue.
The doctor hit him with a club
And charged him one and two.

And so my friend
This is the end,
A warning to the few:
Stay clear of doctors to the end
Or they'll get rid of you.

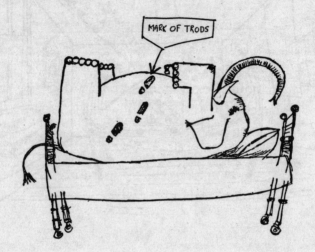

Confined-to-bed Elephant

Contagion

Elephants are contagious!
    Be careful how you tread.
An Elephant that's been trodden on
    Should be confined to bed!

Leopards are contagious too.
    Be careful tiny tots.
They don't give you a temperature
    But lots and lots – of spots.

The Herring is a lucky fish,
    From all disease inured.
Should he be ill when caught at sea;
    Immediately – he's cured!

Round and Round

Small poem based on my daughter's (6) remarks on overhearing me tell her brother Sean (4½) that the world was going round. (Australia, June–July, 1958.)

One day a little boy called Sean
(Age four) became profound.
He asked his dad
If it were true
The world was going round.

'Oh yes, that's true,' his daddy said.
'It goes round night and day.'
'Then doesn't it get tired dad?'
Young Sean was heard to say.

His sister in the bath called out
'What did dad say – what did he?'
He said 'The world is going round.'
Said she 'Well it's making me giddy!'

The ABC

T'was midnight in the schoolroom
And every desk was shut,
When suddenly from the alphabet
Was heard a loud 'Tut-tut!'

Said A to B, 'I don't like C;
His manners are a lack.
For all I ever see of C
Is a semi-circular back!'

'I disagree,' said D to B,
'I've never found C so.
From where I stand, he seems to be
An uncompleted O.'

C was vexed, 'I'm much perplexed,
You criticize my shape.
I'm made like that, to help spell Cat
And Cow and Cool and Cape.'

'He's right,' said E; said F, 'Whoopee!'
Said G, ''Ip, 'ip, 'ooray!'
'You're dropping me,' roared H to G.
'Don't do it please I pray!'

'Out of my way,' LL said to K.
'I'll make poor I look ILL.'
To stop this stunt, J stood in front,
And presto! ILL was JILL.

'U know,' said V, 'that W
Is twice the age of me,
For as Roman V is five
I'm half as young as he.'

X and Y yawned sleepily,
'Look at the time!' they said.
'Let's all get off to beddy byes.'
They did, then, 'Z-z-z.'

or

alternative last verse

X and Y yawned sleepily,
'Look at the time!' they said.
They all jumped in to beddy byes
And the last one in was Z!

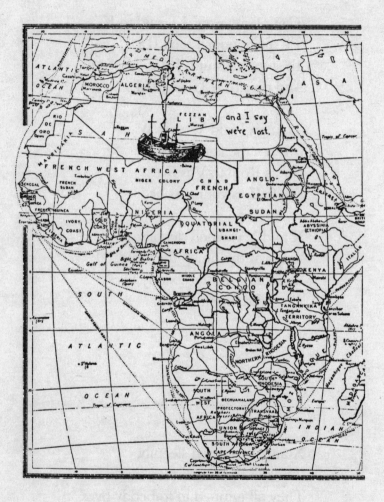

Bump!

Things that go 'bump!' in the night,
Should not really give one a fright.
It's the hole in each ear
That lets in the fear,
That, and the absence of light!

Soldier Freddy

Soldier Freddy
was never ready,
But Soldier Neddy,
unlike Freddy,
Was <u>always</u> ready,
and steady,

Thats why,
When soldier Neddy
Is·outside·Buckingham·Palace·on guard·in·the·
pouring·wind·and·rain·
being·steady·and·ready,
Freddie —
is home in beddy

NOTHING.

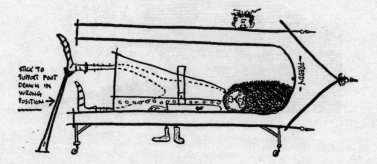

STICK TO
SUPPORT FOOT
DRAWN IN
WRONG
POSITION →

← FREDDY →

Rain

There are holes in the sky
    Where the rain gets in,
But they're ever so small
    That's why rain is thin.

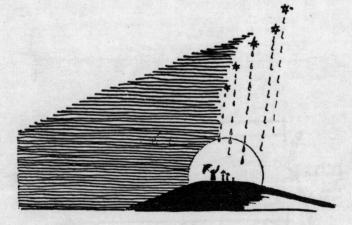

'Roger McGough is a true original and more than one generation would be much the poorer without him' – *The Times Educational Supplement*

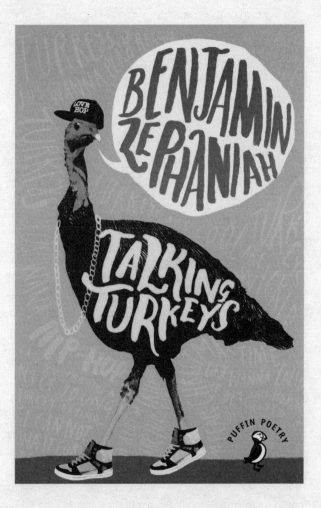

'. . . A collection that works well on the page
and is a delight to read aloud' – *Guardian*

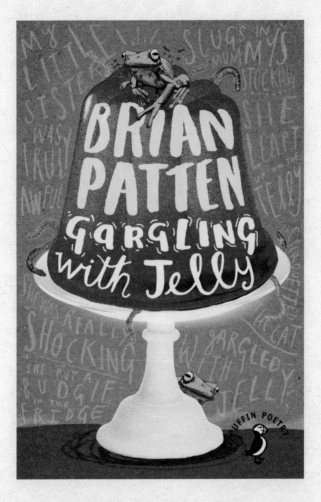

Full of Brian Patten's wonderful wit!

A collection of witty and brilliant poems that
bring our monarchy to life!

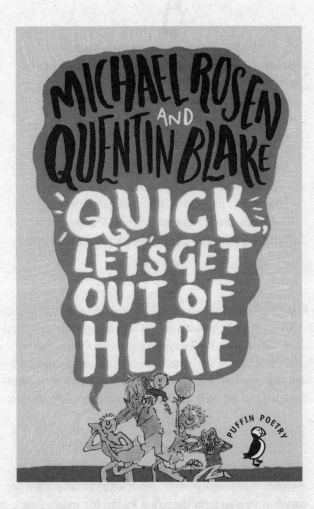

'Michael Rosen is one of our most popular writers
– the champion for every bored, overdrilled,
tested-to-tears pupil in the land' – *The Times*

It all started with a Scarecrow

Puffin is over seventy years old.
Sounds ancient, doesn't it? But Puffin has never been
so lively. We're always on the lookout for the next big
idea, which is how it began all those years ago.

Penguin Books was a big idea from the mind of
a man called Allen Lane, who in 1935 invented
the quality paperback and changed the world.
**And from great Penguins, great Puffins grew,
changing the face of children's books forever.**

The first four Puffin Picture Books were hatched in 1940 and the
first Puffin story book featured a man with broomstick arms called
Worzel Gummidge. In 1967 Kaye Webb, Puffin Editor, started the
Puffin Club, promising to **'make children into readers'**.
She kept that promise and over 200,000 children became devoted
Puffineers through their quarterly instalments of *Puffin Post*.

Many years from now, we hope you'll look back and
remember Puffin with a smile. **No matter what your age
or what you're into, there's a Puffin for everyone.**
The possibilities are endless, but one thing is for sure:
whether it's a picture book or a paperback, a sticker book
or a hardback, **if it's got that little Puffin
on it – it's bound to be good.**

www.puffinbooks.com